DOWN IN THE OCEAN

FROZEN REALMS

BY MELISSA GISH

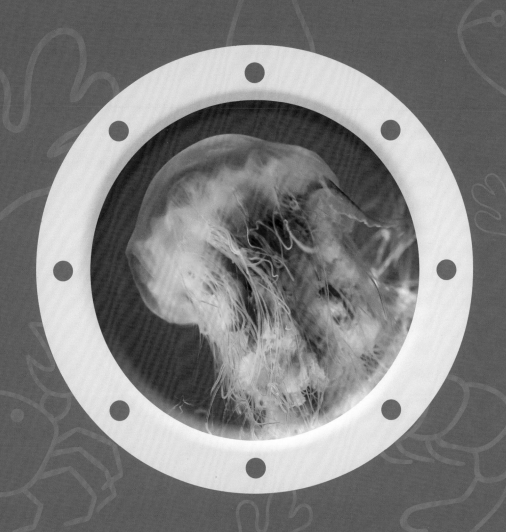

CREATIVE EDUCATION • CREATIVE PAPERBACKS

Published by Creative Education and Creative Paperbacks
P.O. Box 227, Mankato, Minnesota 56002
Creative Education and Creative Paperbacks are imprints of
The Creative Company
www.thecreativecompany.us

Design, production, and illustrations by Chelsey Luther
Art direction by Rita Marshall
Printed in China

Photographs by Alamy (Aurora Photos, Auscape International Pty Ltd, Maik
Brand, Cultura Creative, dieKleinert, Nature Picture Library, Andrey Nekrasov,
Jeff Rotman, Keren Su/China Span, WorldFoto), All-free-download.com,
freevectormaps.com, Getty Images (Design Pics Inc, John Hyde/First Light,
KEENPRESS, Paul Souders/Corbis Documentary, Masa Ushioda/age footstock),
iStockphoto (florencemcginn, Ray Hems, LPETTET, Mlenny, pilipenkoD, Pley, RL-
SPHOTO, Smokhov), Minden Pictures (Tui De Roy, Flip Nicklin, Norbert Wu), Na-
tional Geographic Creative (Paul Nicklen), Shutterstock (Anton Balazh)

Library of Congress Cataloging-in-Publication Data
Names: Gish, Melissa, author.
Title: Frozen realms / Melissa Gish.
Series: Down in the ocean.
Includes bibliographical references and index.
Summary: Explore the coldest regions of the world's oceans and learn about the
life forms that dwell there. First-person accounts from scientists answer import-
ant questions about polar-sea creatures and how they survive.
Identifiers: LCCN 2017027664 / ISBN 978-1-60818-997-7 (hardcover) / ISBN 978-
1-62832-552-2 (pbk) / ISBN 978-1-64000-026-1 (eBook)

Subjects: LCSH: 1. Marine animals—Polar regions—Juvenile literature. 2. Marine
ecology—Polar regions—Juvenile literature. 3. Polar regions—Juvenile literature.
Classification: LCC QH95.56.G57 2018 / DDC 591.770911—dc23

CCSS: RI.4.1, 2, 7; RI.5.1, 2, 3, 8; RST.6-8.1, 2, 5, 6, 8

First Edition HC 9 8 7 6 5 4 3 2 1
First Edition PBK 9 8 7 6 5 4 3 2 1

TABLE OF CONTENTS

WELCOME TO THE FROZEN REALMS

At the top of the world, massive sheets of ice float on frigid seawater. Some of this Arctic sea ice is more than 65 feet (19.8 m) thick. At the bottom of the world lies Antarctica. Here, the Atlantic, Pacific, and Indian oceans meet to form the Southern Ocean. The Antarctic continent is surrounded by vast ice shelves.

Below the polar ice, the water is 28 °F (-2.2 °C). It may seem as though nothing could survive in this frigid environment. Yet corals, sponges, sea stars, octopuses, shrimp, fish, and marine worms are just some of the creatures that thrive here. With every dive into the frozen realms, scientists encounter new **species**. They haven't even been able to identify or name all their discoveries yet!

1

INFINITE WONDERS

Scientists first explored the deep sea beneath the North Pole in 2007. Today, most Arctic waters remain unexplored. Near Alaska, the Bering Sea is home to some of the largest underwater canyons on Earth. Few people have glimpsed the amazing animals in these deep-water canyons. Antarctica is the largest ice mass on the planet. In 2015, scientists drilled through nearly half a mile (0.8 km) of ice on the Ross Ice Shelf. In the near-freezing water below, a remote-controlled camera spotted fish!

The polar seas are home to abundant creatures, from tiny plankton to huge marine mammals. Life underwater is more rich and diverse than anyone had ever imagined. At the heart of this ecosystem are tiny shrimp-like krill. These animals are vital to the polar ecosystems. They are food for everything from fish and squid to seals and whales.

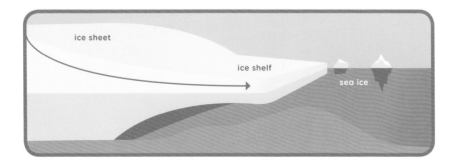

White-blooded fish

There are 25 species of icefish in the Southern Ocean. They are the only vertebrates without hemoglobin in their blood. This substance carries oxygen throughout the body. Hemoglobin also makes blood red. So icefish have colorless blood. Their bodies even look like ice!

Lions of the sea

The lion's mane jellyfish is the world's largest jellyfish. A jellyfish body is called a bell. The lion's mane's bell can be wider than six feet (1.8 m) across. It has eight clusters of sticky tentacles. Each cluster can contain more than 100 tentacles. These tentacles can be more than 100 feet (30.5 m) long.

ASK A 🐙 SCIENTIST

What do you think is the most interesting creature that lives in the polar sea?

For me, the most interesting creatures that live in the polar sea are the Antarctic icefish. These fish live without oxygen transporting hemoglobin. They produce antifreeze proteins that prevent their blood and tissues from freezing. Some of them die of heat stress at only 57.2 °F (14 °C).

— Dr. Markus Frederich, Marine Scientist, University of New England

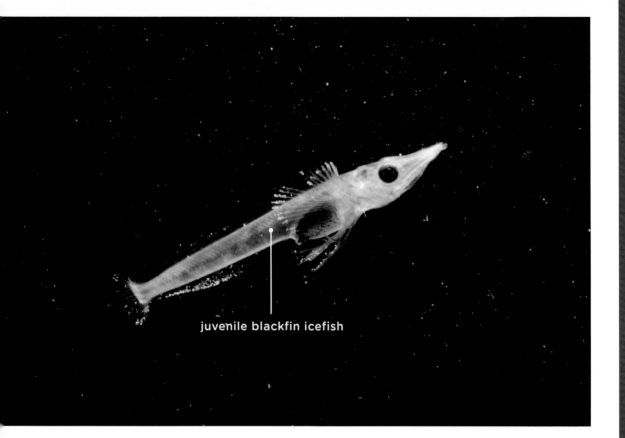

juvenile blackfin icefish

lion's mane jellyfish

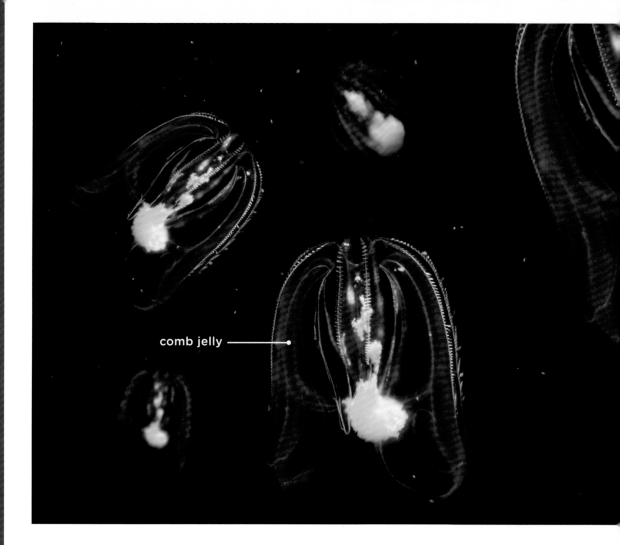

comb jelly

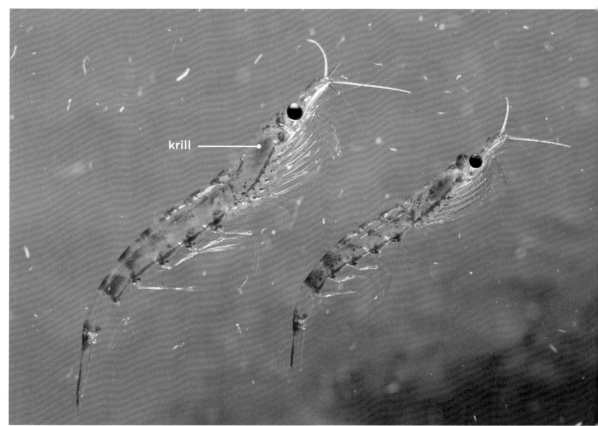

krill

All dressed up

Ribbon seals live in the Sea of Okhotsk and the Bering Sea. These seals are black with four white bands. Ribbon seals live alone. They eat about 20 pounds (9.1 kg) of squid, octopus, and fish every day. Their main predators are polar bears and killer whales.

Lights and color

Comb jellies have no bones. They have eight rows of comblike structures that flutter. This is how they swim. They are bioluminescent, which means they can glow. Most comb jellies dangle long tentacles below their bodies. Copepods and other small crustaceans stick to the tentacles. Comb jellies eat jellyfish, too.

11

ASK A  SCIENTIST

What is your favorite animal in the Southern Ocean?

My favorite animal is the Antarctic krill. I have investigated the **ecology** and **physiology** of these fascinating small animals for many years. The Antarctic krill play a critical role in the Southern Ocean **food web**. They are the primary prey for many predators. And they are being **commercially** fished.
— Dr. Kendra L. Daly, Biological Oceanographer, University of South Florida

humpback whale

2

EAT OR BE EATEN

Summer sunlight feeds algae growing under thin ice and on shallow seafloors. This makes the algae bloom. It feeds millions of microscopic organisms. In turn, these creatures feed larger plankton and krill that drift with the currents. From here, the fight for survival continues up the food chain. Many invertebrates anchor themselves to the seabed. They capture passing prey. Other polar sea creatures are skilled hunters. Seals capture penguins in the water. Polar bears nab seals at holes in the ice. Greenland sharks are known to eat polar bears!

POLAR SEA FOOD CHAIN

herbivores and omnivores

producers

carnivores

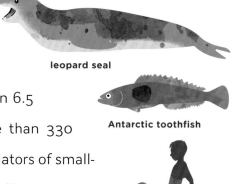

leopard seal

Antarctic toothfish

10-year-old

Predator and prey

Antarctic toothfish are the largest fish in the Ross Sea. They grow to more than 6.5 feet (2 m) long. They can weigh more than 330 pounds (150 kg). Toothfish are fierce predators of smaller fish. But much bigger Weddell seals, killer whales, and sperm whales hunt Antarctic toothfish.

Mighty marine mammal

Leopard seals have front biting teeth that are one inch (2.5 cm) long. These seals are brutal hunters. They bash penguins and smaller seals on the ground until they are dead. Leopard seals weigh more than polar bears. They are the second-biggest seal species. Only the southern elephant seal is larger.

ASK A SCIENTIST

What is a behavior that helps an animal get food under the ice?

Weddell seals often dive from isolated holes under a broad plain of sea ice six feet (1.8 m) thick. Below the ice, it is dark. The seals may travel two to three miles (3.2–4.8 km) under the ice to another hole. How they do that is uncertain. They may travel that far, even in winter, when it is dark for one to two months.
— Dr. Gerald Kooyman, Marine Biologist, Scripps Institution of Oceanography

leopard seal

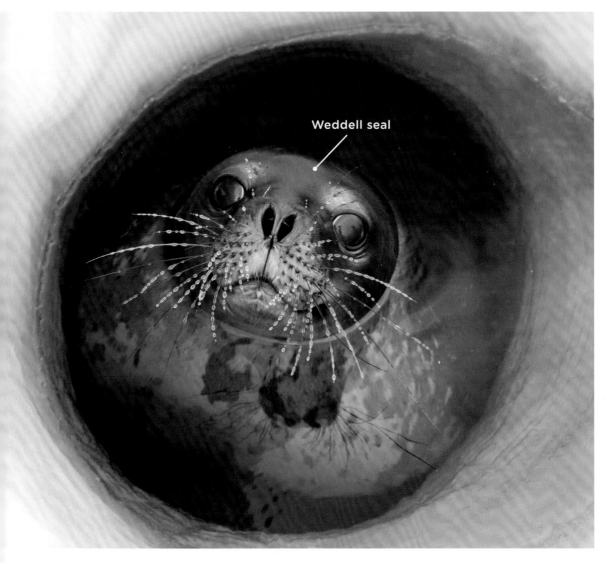

Weddell seal

sea spider

Spiders in the sea

Spiders are classified as arachnids. Sea spiders are not true spiders, though. They have eight legs and four eyes. Some species eat algae. Most attack corals, sponges, and other tiny invertebrates. They have three teeth that bite holes in prey. Then they suck out the prey's body fluids and soft tissue.

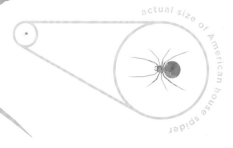

sea spider

actual size of American house spider

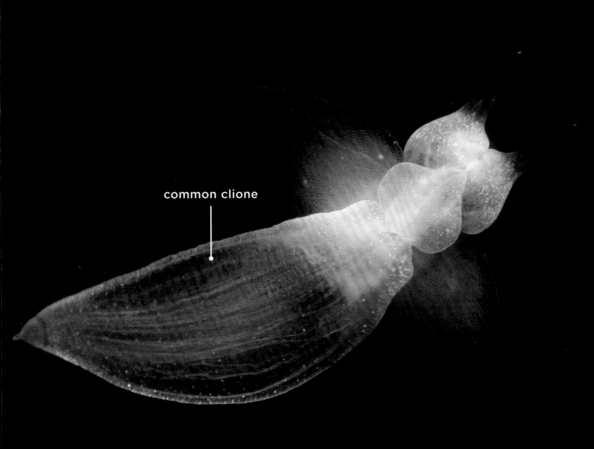

common clione

ASK A 🐙 SCIENTIST

What is an interesting ocean predator?

My favorite is the clione (*klee-OH-nee*). These sea slugs live in the chilly waters around the Arctic and Antarctic. They swim around by paddling with specialized fins. It almost looks like they're flying through the water on tiny wings, earning them the nickname "sea angels." But don't be fooled by the name. These angels are actually hungry predators on the hunt for sea snails!

— Alexander Carsh, Marine Ecologist, San Diego State University

humpback whale

barnacle

SPECIAL RELATIONSHIPS

Life in the polar seas is richer than scientists once realized. They are still trying to understand how creatures survive in this harsh habitat. Cooperation among organisms can be a means of survival. Many creatures form special relationships. One such relationship is commensalism. It involves one animal using another to get something useful. Neither creature is harmed. Another type of relationship is parasitism. One organism, called a parasite, takes something from an animal called the host. Parasites can make hosts sick or even cause their death.

19

TYPES OF SYMBIOTIC RELATIONSHIPS

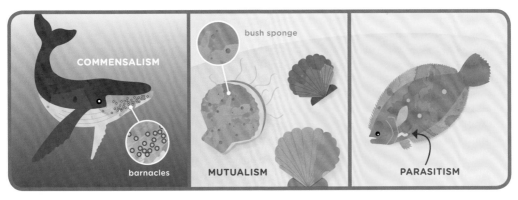

COMMENSALISM

barnacles

bush sponge

MUTUALISM

PARASITISM

Hitching a ride

Bush sponges attach themselves to scallops. The sponges are lightweight. They are like slender strands. So the scallops do not shake them off. As the scallops swim, the sponges feed on bits of food floating in the water.

Little bloodsuckers

Cod worms are copepods. They attach themselves to the gills of fish in the cold northern seas. These parasites mostly attack cod, lumpuckers, and flounders. They drive a needle-like mouthpart into the fish. Then they suck the fish's blood. This can slowly kill the fish.

20

ASK A  SCIENTIST

Can sea creatures get worms like dogs and cats do?

Yes, they can. Marine worms can be obtained from the food they eat, such as plankton or other marine animals. Some parasitic worms can swim through the water column, penetrate the skin of their host, and then travel to the appropriate tissue or organ within the fish or crustacean. Parasites are found in virtually all living animals, occupying various tissues and organs in their host.

— Dr. Nancy Smith, Marine Scientist, Eckerd College

bush sponge

spiny scallop

sea slug

DEPTH ZONES

SUNLIGHT ZONE *(Epipelagic)*

TWILIGHT ZONE *(Mesopelagic)*   650 ft

3,300 ft

MIDNIGHT ZONE
(Bathypelagic)

9,800 ft

proboscis worm

ABYSSAL ZONE
(Abyssopelagic)

Cleanup crew

Proboscis worms are important in Antarctic waters. They clean up dead animals that float or fall to the seafloor. They can dive more than two miles (3.2 km) deep. They grow up to 6.5 feet (2 m) long but weigh less than a baseball.

23

ASK A 🐙 SCIENTIST

The polar seas are filled with invertebrates. Which is your favorite?

My favorite marine invertebrate is whichever one I am looking at at the moment! There is something fascinating about each. It could be shape, color, behavior, or how it interacts with plants and animals. If I had to pick, I would say that marine gastropods (snails) are my favorite for sheer diversity of species and ecological habits.

— Dr. Jonathan Geller, Invertebrate Zoologist, Moss Landing Marine Laboratories

harp seal pup

FAMILY LIFE

Reproduction in the polar seas is typically seasonal. In late winter, many marine mammals gather to mate. In the spring, they give birth on floating ice. Many polar fish, such as Atlantic cod, also reproduce from winter to early spring. Atlantic cod lay as many as 9 million eggs per year. Some fish, such as Greenland sharks, give birth to fully formed offspring. Corals and sponges split to create copies of themselves. Comb jellies have both male and female reproductive organs. They can create offspring by themselves.

POLAR SEA REPRODUCTION

OVOVIVIPAROUS   VIVIPAROUS   OVIPAROUS

Icebreakers

In winter, ice may completely cover the Arctic sea. Walruses need to make breathing holes. They can use their heads to break holes in ice that is eight inches (20.3 cm) thick. Walruses have their babies on floating ice. Without this ice, the babies would drown.

Fish on the beach

Capelins are small Arctic fish. They are eaten by whales, seals, larger fish, and seabirds. Capelins eat plankton around ice sheets. In spring, mature capelins migrate to shallow shore-lines to reproduce. Some capelins throw themselves onto beaches. Then they lay their eggs among pebbles.

ASK A 🐙 SCIENTIST

What is the fiercest animal that lives in the sea around Antarctica?

Killer whales are considered the top predator. In the Southern Ocean, one type of killer whale eats only seals, and another eats only fish. However, I think leopard seals are the fiercest predator. They prey on a wider variety of animals, such as krill, fish, squid, penguins, and seals. They also are known to attack humans.
— Dr. Kendra L. Daly, Biological Oceanographer, University of South Florida

walrus

capelin

ASK A SCIENTIST

Do you have a favorite ocean animal that lives under the ice?

Weddell seals make their living and find their mates below the ice and rest on top of the ice. They are the only mammal that lives near the continent [Antarctica] year round. During their sojourn in Antarctic waters, they may dive to 2,411 feet (735 m). At other times, they may hold their breath for 82 minutes while traveling below the ice.

— Dr. Gerald Kooyman, Marine Biologist, Scripps Institution of Oceanography

Drifting offspring

Male and female crinoids release their reproductive cells into the water. The cells mix to create fertilized eggs. The eggs hatch into tiny larvae. They drift on the currents for a few days. Then they sink. They glue themselves to the seabed, where they grow. Some adult crinoids swim along the floor in search of food.

crinoid

ice pack

5

OCEAN MYSTERIES

Earth is covered by almost 10 million square miles (25.9 million sq km) of sea ice. Until recently, no one knew what—if anything—lived beneath the ice. In 1902, a sailor named Willy Heinrich became the first person to dive under the ice in Antarctica. But he wasn't studying marine life. He was repairing a ship. It wasn't until 1957 that marine scientist Dr. John S. Bunt dove into the Antarctic water to study algae. In 1974, Dr. Joseph MacInnis became the first person to dive under the North Pole.

To this day, few people have seen the depths of the polar seas. The invention of submersible vehicles has allowed greater exploration of the ocean. But the polar seas are unlike any other oceans on the planet. Thousands of unique organisms call the icy waters around the poles their home.

emperor penguin

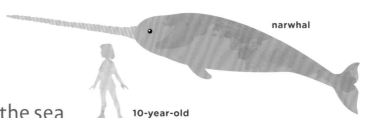

narwhal

Unicorns of the sea

10-year-old

Narwhals are related to beluga whales. They have one long tusk growing from their upper jaw. They live in the Arctic Ocean. They eat squid and fish, including Arctic cod and Greenland halibut. They can dive nearly 5,000 feet (1,524 m), holding their breath.

Icy underwater dragons

There are 19 species of Antarctic dragonfish. Some are stout and muscular. Others are slender and graceful. Dragonfish have many teeth that vary in size. Scientists believe dragonfish teeth are replaced when they break or fall out. Dragonfish eat krill, copepods, crustaceans, and worms.

34

ASK A SCIENTIST

Are there coral reefs in cold places, like around Alaska?

Yes, there are. Alaska has some very beautiful coral gardens and a type of soft coral called the Red Tree Coral. It can grow several feet tall. In Alaska and other places where the water is very cold, deep-sea corals can live at shallower depths than in warmer regions like Florida. This makes them easier to study.

— Dr. Sandra Brooke, Oceanographer, Florida State University

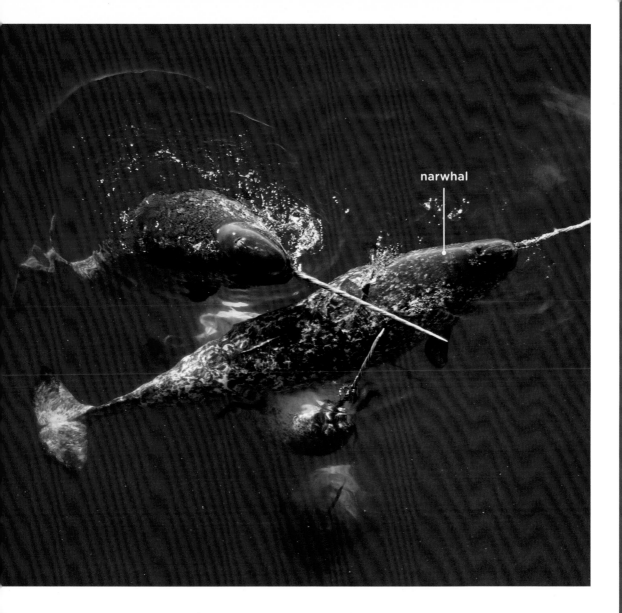

narwhal

juvenile deepwater dragonfish

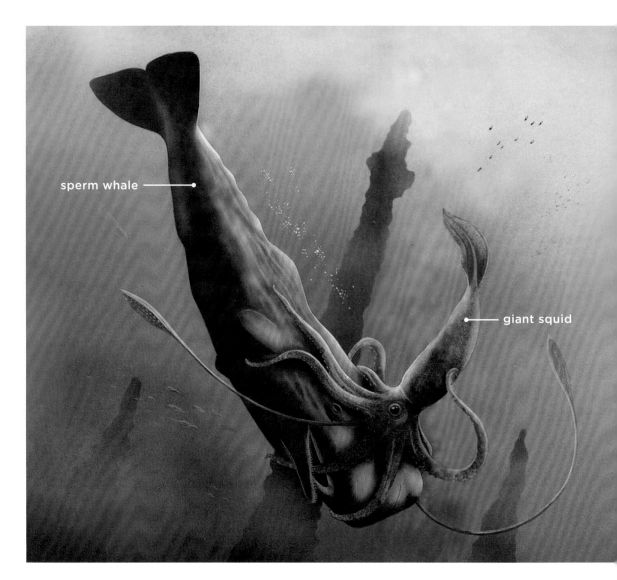

sperm whale

giant squid

Greenland shark

Deep-sea battles

Sperm whales hunt colossal squid around Antarctica. The squid are believed to be nearly as long as a school bus. Sperm whales have sharp, seven-inch-long (17.8 cm) teeth. Scientists believe these animals do battle. Sperm whales' bodies often bear scars from squid's sharp claws.

Scavenger shark

The Greenland shark barely moves around its Arctic habitat. Unlike many other sharks, it does not hunt. It scavenges. This means it eats dead animals. It swallows dead fish and penguins. It also bites chunks of flesh off dead seals and whales.

ASK A SCIENTIST

What is the most interesting thing people have found deep in the Arctic Ocean?

Ash deposits from explosive volcanic eruptions. It was thought that this was not possible. That is, it was believed that volcanoes on the deep Arctic seafloor could not erupt explosively. So this discovery was a shock. It has changed the way we think about the Arctic seafloor volcanoes. [Dr. Sohn's research team made this discovery in 2007.]

— Dr. Robert A. Sohn, Geophysicist, Woods Hole Oceanographic Institution

SOUTH AMERICA

ANTARCTICA

Bransfield
Strait

4

Weddell Sea

2

3

ANTARCTIC
PENINSULA

Bellingshausen Sea

Lar
Ice S

KEY

1 Ushuaia, Argentina

2 Orne Harbor

3 Paradise Harbor

4 Deception Island

TRUE-LIFE POLAR SEAS ADVENTURE

KAYAKING AROUND ANTARCTICA

Geoff Head loves kayaking. A kayak is a type of canoe. It has a small opening in the top where the kayak-er sits. One special place that Geoff wanted to kayak was Antarctica. To get there, Geoff boarded a ship in Ushuaia, Argentina. From the southern tip of South America, the ship carried Geoff across the rough waters of the Southern

Ocean. On the morning of the third day, the ship reached Orne Harbor on the Antarctic Peninsula. Here, the sea was calm.

Geoff put on a special suit to help him stay dry and warm. Then his kayak was lowered into the water. Other kayakers joined him. Bits of ice floated on the still water. Rocky ridges and outcroppings covered the frozen shoreline. Geoff dipped his oar in the water and set off. On a nearby ice floe, a crab-eater seal gazed lazily at the kayakers. Chinstrap and gentoo penguins chattered from the shore.

On his third day in Antarctica, Geoff traveled around Paradise Harbor. Huge icebergs reflected the sun's light, appearing blue. Geoff saw a leopard seal and its offspring, called a pup, resting on an ice floe. Then a small group of killer whales swam right beneath him. They began spyhopping. This is when a killer whale pops straight out of the water and then silently slips back down. It is checking the surface for prey. The killer whales spotted the leopard seals and headed toward the ice floe. Geoff watched as one killer whale rushed toward the ice. The resulting wave tipped the floe. The seal pup tumbled into the water. Another killer whale grabbed the pup and pulled it underwater. Geoff had just witnessed a harsh reminder of the Antarctic food web.

Before Geoff's Antarctic adventure ended, he wanted to do something a little crazy. He went to the beach at Deception Island. He put on only swim trunks. Then he dashed into the icy ocean for a quick polar plunge! "It was invigorating!" Geoff said.

Adélie penguin

6

UNDER PRESSURE

Earth's polar regions are special. But the future of these eco-systems is uncertain. The greatest threat to the polar seas is climate change. West Antarctica is one of the fastest-warming areas on the planet. Temperature change has led to a decrease in algae. This has led to a decline in krill. Fewer krill has meant a decreased food supply for many other species, including Adé-lie penguins and various fish.

In the Arctic, vast areas of ocean that once remained fro-zen all summer are melted. This makes life for marine mam-mals difficult. They need ice and snow to raise their offspring. In addition, commercial fishing in Arctic waters is leading to declines in sea life populations. Human activities around the world affect the polar seas. We must consider ways to repair Earth's frozen realms. We must protect the amazing creatures that live down in the ocean.

ice calving

ASK A 🐙 SCIENTIST

Is it too late to stop the polar icecaps from melting?

We put excess carbon dioxide into the atmosphere. Even if we stopped right now, our kids and grandkids are still going to have to deal with the energy that all that carbon dioxide will put into the ocean. Polar ice is still going to melt. Sea levels are going to continue to rise, no matter what. The only way to stop that would be to take carbon dioxide out of the atmosphere. And even then, we don't know if we can stop the already unstable ice from melting. A lot of the forces that we need to harness for the future are not being harnessed. But I believe that we're smart enough to use the brains that we have. I think that education and information outweigh ignorance.

— Dr. Jim White, Geological Scientist, University of Colorado Boulder

New opportunity for destruction

Climate change is melting ice in the northern Barents Sea. This has allowed commercial fishing vessels to operate there for the first time. Huge nets dragged along the seafloor have destroyed deep-water coral reefs. They have killed many rare animals such as bowhead whales and Greenland sharks.

beluga whale

Largest Canadian marine protected area

In 2017, the Canadian government established its largest marine protected area. About 42,085 square miles (109,000 sq km) in and around Lancaster Sound will protect fish, beluga and bowhead whales, and other marine mammals from commercial fishing and the oil and gas industry.

RUSSIA

ALASKA

Zhemchug Canyon

BERING SEA

Pribilof Canyon

ASK A 🐙 SCIENTIST

What is an example of how commercial fishing affects Alaska?

Pribilof Canyon and Zhemchug Canyon in the Bering Sea are incredibly productive canyons. Zhemchug is the largest underwater canyon in the world. These canyons and the species that are thriving there are absolutely essential for the health of the entire Bering Sea ecosystem. I think if we don't afford these habitats some protection from fishing, we're going to see continued declines in species we harvest. This includes marine mammals for some people. We're going to continue to see declines in some of our target commercial catches as well.

— Dr. Michelle Ridgway, Marine Ecologist, Alaska Deep Ocean Science Institute

GLOSSARY

climate change
the gradual increase in Earth's temperature that causes changes in the planet's atmosphere, environments, and long-term weather conditions

commercially
being used for business and to gain a profit rather than for personal reasons

crustaceans
animals with no backbone that have a shell covering a soft body

ecology
the study of the relationships of organisms living together in an environment

ecosystem
a community of organisms that live together in balance

food web
a system in nature in which living things depend on one other for food

gills
body parts that extract oxygen from water

invertebrates
animals that lack a backbone, including shellfish, insects, and worms

larvae
the form some juvenile animals take before changing into adults

mammals
warm-blooded animals that have a backbone and hair or fur, give birth to live young, and produce milk to feed their young

physiology
the scientific study of the functions and parts of living organisms' bodies

plankton
algae and animals that drift or float in the ocean, many of which are microscopic

species
a group of living beings with shared characteristics and the ability to reproduce with one another

tentacles
slender, flexible limbs in an animal, used for grasping, moving about, or feeling

vertebrates
animals that have a backbone

SELECTED BIBLIOGRAPHY

Australian Government. "Wildlife." Department of the Environment and Energy. Australian Antarctic Division. http://www.antarctica.gov.au/about-antarctica/wildlife.

Earle, Sylvia, narrator. *Antarctic Ocean*. National Geographic. https://video.nationalgeographic.com/video/oceans-antarctica.

Earle, Sylvia, narrator. *Arctic Ocean*. National Geographic. https://video.nationalgeographic.com/video/oceans-arctic.

Lowen, James. *Antarctic Wildlife: A Visitor's Guide*. Princeton, N.J.: Princeton University Press, 2011.

Palumbi, Stephen R., and Anthony R. Palumbi. *The Extreme Life of the Sea*. Princeton, N.J.: Princeton University Press, 2014.

Sale, Richard. *A Complete Guide to Arctic Wildlife*. Ontario, Canada: Firefly Books, 2006.

Note: Every effort has been made to ensure that any websites listed above were active at the time of publication. However, because of the nature of the Internet, it is impossible to guarantee that these sites will remain active indefinitely or that their contents will not be altered.

INDEX